I0800650

CATHOLIC STORIES FOR BOYS AND GIRLS

Volumes 1–4

Student Workbook

TAN Books
Gastonia, North Carolina

Catholic Stories for Boy and Girls Volumes 1–4 Student Workbook © 2022 TAN Books

All rights reserved. With the exception of short excerpts used in critical review, no part of this work may be reproduced, transmitted, or stored in any form whatsoever, without the prior written permission of the publisher. Creation, exploitation, and distribution of any unauthorized editions of this work, in any format in existence now or in the future—including but not limited to text, audio, and video—is prohibited without the prior written permission of the publisher.

Cover design by Jordan Avery

Interior Images: Santa Maria Ship by Intelligent Design / Shutterstock (16), Our Lady of Miraculous Medal by Immaculate / Shutterstock (26), Vector Black and White Circus Tent by Lexi Claus / Shutterstock (54), Jesus Christ Feeds People by Keya / Shutterstock (72), Saint Vincent de Paul - © TheCatholicKid.com, printed here with permission (95).

ISBN: 978-1-5051-2715-7

Published in the United States by
TAN Books
PO Box 269
Gastonia, NC 28053
www.TANBooks.com

Printed in the United States of America

CATHOLIC STORIES FOR BOYS AND GIRLS

Volumes 1–4

Student Workbook

Contents

Publisher's Preface . . . . *vii*

Catholic Stories for Boys and Girls Volume 1

The Best Deed 3

The Wreath of Flowers 9

Pedro of the Water Jars 13

The Little Dove of Our Lady 19

The Great Gift of Our Lady 23

Black Robe 27

Catholic Stories for Boys and Girls Volume 2

Ottawanta. 33

Elizabeth Bayley Seton 37

Anina 41

Silver Wings 45

John Philip 51

Catholic Stories for Boys and Girls Volume 3

Begga's Bracelet. 57

In the Tower of London 61

Joseph. 65

Louise. 69

Catholic Stories for Boys and Girls Volume 4

The Dawn of Spring 75

The Land of Erin 79

The Flowery Kingdom 83

The Lion Tamer 87

A Shepherd and His Sheep 91

Publisher's Preface

Dear Parent,

These workbooks are designed to accompany the stories found in the children's books *Catholic Stories for Boys and Girls*. Each of the books in this four volume series contains four, five, or six short stories. These short stories are meant to enlighten the minds of your children. The stories can be enjoyed by children of any age, and these workbooks are flexible enough to be used throughout all of elementary school.

Each chapter of this workbook focuses on one story and contains five components: **Key terms** let the child know about the main characters, locations, or concepts in the story. There is a short **vocabulary** section. The child ought to be able to come up with some definition for the vocabulary word found in bold based on context clues. If your child needs help, please don't hesitate to provide it! Some of the vocabulary terms are words your child has probably never seen. There is a list of **comprehension questions** for each chapter, and the answers are found by doing a careful reading of the text. Finally, each chapter has a **sequencing** section. Your child should put the events in the story in order from first to last. The sequencing practice helps children become careful readers and listeners by ordering their thinking.

There are many additional **activities** in each chapter of the workbook. These range from true/false questions to word searches, crossword puzzles, and illustrations. The most important of these additional activities are the reflection questions and the retelling components.

Reflection questions allow the child to have a conversation with mom and dad. A prompt is included to help the child think carefully about how the story might relate to his or her own life. The characters in these stories face many challenges, overcome hardships, and always have their eyes set on Jesus and Mary. Even though your children might be young, and blessed to not have to think about martyrdom, it is good for them to be thinking about the challenges they might face and the little sacrifices they can make each day.

The retelling component is another important skill. It provides children with an opportunity to share their learning in their own way. Retelling teaches children to organize their thoughts, which leads to logical thinking in life. As parents, we learn how our children think and process information by practicing retelling often.

In general, after hearing or reading a passage, a child retells the story in his or her own words. The way you approach the task of retelling may look different than another homeschooling family. You might even use a different method for each child! For a young child, you might read one or two sections from one of the stories in the book and then ask for a retelling. For an older child, it might be reasonable to expect a fairly solid retelling after reading the whole story, including correct sequencing of events. Children have a wonderful habit of attention. They retain much more than one might expect! During the retelling, give the child time to speak and try to avoid interrupting them. Sometimes a child might need a prompt, but these prompts should be rare!

You might consider writing down or typing your child's narration as they speak. Write down word for word what they say. Children should use complete sentences during a retelling. A retelling should not read like an outline; it should read like a carefully crafted story! When the child finishes their retelling, you might have them copy some or all of it to see the modeled spelling and grammar. Copying provides extra practice in handwriting and reinforces those grammar and spelling skills you might not yet be focused on while they are so young. They might color an illustration too. You have flexibility with this practice.

In all of these activities, what you do and how you do it is up to you! If you are working through these books with a kindergartener or first grader, you might be doing many of these activities orally. Many younger elementary children aren't strong readers, so even reading the stories may be beyond their skill level. That's okay! Read the story to them, or take turns reading. Ask the child questions from the workbook, and you can write down their responses. When your child is able to write their own responses, then consider adding that practice to their workload.

May your time with these beautiful stories be richly blessed, and may your family grow in love for Christ through your homeschooling.

In Christ,
TAN Books

Catholic Stories for Boys and Girls

Volume 1

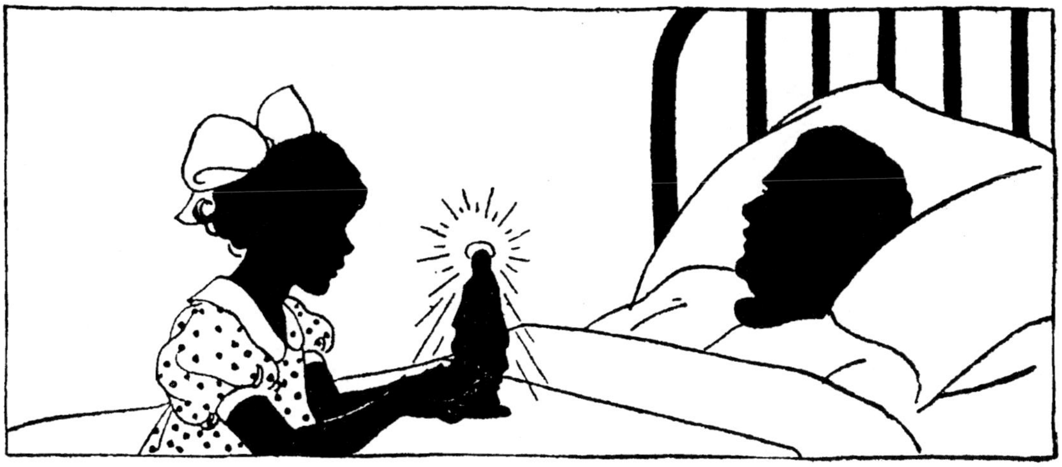

The Best Deed

Key Terms

These are important people, places, and things you should remember from this story.

Sister Rose - Taught Confirmation class and planned to give a prize to the child who performed the best deed before Confirmation.

Catherine Duffy - Student in Confirmation class who met the poor sick man and helped save his soul.

The Poor Sick Man - Sick man who believed he was unworthy of God's love and mercy. Met Catherine Duffy before his death.

Confirmation - The sacrament through which the Holy Ghost comes to us in a special way and enables us to profess our faith as strong and perfect Christians and soldiers of Jesus Christ.

Confession - Telling our sins to Jesus through a priest in order to obtain forgiveness.

Vocabulary

Read the sentences below and note the use of the word in ***bold****. Write a definition or synonym for this word by considering its context.*

1. What shall I do for a good **deed**?

2. The white **cornettes** made Catherine think of white birds flying.

3. In her room, there was a pretty little **altar**.

4. Father gave him **absolution**.

5. Through this holy **unction** and His tender mercy, may Our Lord forgive you.

Comprehension Questions

To better understand this story, ask yourself these questions and write down your answers using complete sentences.

1. Sister Rose promised the children that the child who performed the best deed before Confirmation Day would earn the statue of Our Lady. What did Sister Rose tell the students to do to tell her about their good deed?

2. Catherine Duffy considered what good deed she might do to earn the statue of Our Lady. Everyone in her family had a different suggestion for her. What did she decide to do for her good deed?

3. Catherine's father, Doctor Duffy, worked as a doctor at Saint Mary's Hospital. Catherine enjoyed visiting the hospital with him. What is the name of the religious order of sisters that also worked at the hospital?

4. The day after Catherine met the poor sick man, she told him to go to confession. He told her he would not go to confession because he had been too bad and God had no use for him. When was the last time the poor sick man went to confession?

5. Catherine told the poor sick man a story from Scripture to remind him of God's mercy. What story did she tell him and why?

____

____

____

6. After the poor sick man went to confession and received Holy Communion, what other sacrament did he receive?

____

____

____

7. What did Catherine tell Sister Rose about in her letter? Did she stick to her sacrifice of giving up candy?

____

____

____

8. Who won the statue of Our Lady? Why?

____

____

____

Sequencing

Number the following statements in the same order they occurred in the story.

___ Catherine brought the poor sick man her Stations of the Cross pictures.
___ Catherine brought the poor sick man her statue of the Sacred Heart.
___ Catherine overheard the poor sick man cursing and asked him to repent.
___ Catherine told the poor sick man that he should go to confession and he told her he had not been since his First Holy Communion.

Number the following statements in the same order they occurred in the story.

___ Catherine gave her perfume to the poor sick man so he could pour it on Our Lord's feet.
___ The poor sick man died, but kissed the Miraculous Medal just before he passed.
___ The poor sick man went to confession and received the Anointing of the Sick.
___ Sister Alice gave Catherine a Miraculous Medal to pin on the poor sick man.

Activity - Word Search

The following is an optional activity used to help your comprehension of the text. Answer the questions from The Best Deed *and locate the answers in the word search. Note: the words also appear horizontally.*

1. ____________ is the sacrament that Catherine and her classmates were preparing for.
2. Just before the poor sick man died, he received the __________ of the Sick.
3. Catherine had a little ________ in her room where she prayed to Jesus.
4. Sister Rose gave __________ the statue of Our Lady after the Confirmation.
5. The poor sick man was anointed with holy oil during __________.
6. Sister Rose wanted the students to focus on doing a good ________ before they were confirmed.
7. Catherine desperately hoped for the poor sick man to go to _________ before he died.
8. One of the items Catherine brought the poor sick man was a ________ of the Sacred Heart.
9. The Sisters of Charity wore ________ on their heads.
10. One of the prayers Catherine prayed with the poor sick man was the ________ of the Cross.

Deed
Statue
Catherine
Confession
Stations
Altar
Confirmation
Unction
Anointing
Cornettes

L O O F D T Z Z L U N H C V N
H Q X H U Y A N O I N T I N G
S C N N A S V V F D L C Z V Q
T A B C L X T W W Q D O S Y D
A T C B T K D A R C U N A K E
T H C O A J A O T X B F O D E
I E A O R T K I W U Y I Q F D
O R E T N N E T C O E R W J G
N I T K D F E S Y C A M B P I
S N O X X O E T U L W A K O R
F E X Q D U K S T Q V T Y D R
R B V Y F X X R S E K I M C U
V L U G A F T S V I S O H Q F
M H D X L J G E J N O N U Q Q
U N C T I O N A D F C N V G B

Activity - Reflection

Discuss with your mom or dad. If you are old enough to write out your response, use the space provided.

Catherine told the poor sick man to say the words "My Jesus, mercy" when he was tempted to curse. When you feel tempted to sin, how can you call upon Jesus to help you be good? Do you say a little prayer like Catherine does? What prayer do you say?

The Wreath of Flowers

Key Terms

These are important people, places, and things you should remember from this story.

Angelo - Boy who was healed by Our Lady and later became a Dominican brother. Met two robbers in the woods and saved their souls.

Fathers and Brothers of Saint Dominic - Religious order founded by Saint Dominic.

Father James - Dominican priest who helped Angelo understand his sadness and change his perspective about pleasing Our Lady.

Brother Joseph - Angelo's traveling companion. Helped save the souls of the two robbers in the woods.

Vocabulary

Read the sentences below and note the use of the word in ***bold****. Write a definition or synonym for this word by considering its context.*

1. **Jack Frost** never bit his nose.

2. They did not see the two men all in black coming **softly** behind them.

3. They lifted their knives to **strike**.

4. They dropped their knives and **hung** their heads.

5. He showed them the **Crucifix**.

Comprehension Questions

To better understand this story, ask yourself these questions and write down your answers using complete sentences.

1. When Angelo was sick for three weeks, his mother was desperate for his healing. What did she do to help him become well?

____

____

2. What was Angelo's daily practice to honor Our Lady?

____

____

3. Brother Angelo was sad during his time with the Brothers of Saint Dominic. He and Father James talked about why he was sad. Why was Angelo sad? What did Father James suggest Angelo do to feel happy again?

____

____

4. The two men that were going to rob and kill Brother Angelo and Brother Joseph saw a vision just as they were about to strike. Describe the first vision they saw.

____

____

5. After Brother Angelo and Brother Joseph finished praying the rosary, Brother Angelo suggested they pray another for men who do not love Our Lady. Describe the vision the two bad men saw when the brothers were praying their second rosary. What did the men think about as they saw the vision?

____

____

6. How did Brother Angelo save the souls of the two bad men? What did he say and teach them?

____

____

Sequencing

Number the following statements in the same order they occurred in the story.

___ The long winter made Angelo feel sad because he could not make a wreath for Our Lady.
___ Angelo's illness was healed when his mother brought him before a statue of Our Lady and begged for his healing.
___ Father James gave Angelo a rosary to pray to cheer him up.
___ Angelo decided that he needed to join the Brothers of Saint Dominic.
___ Angelo spent each night picking flowers for Our Lady to make a wreath.

Number the following statements in the same order they occurred in the story.

___ The robbers nearly killed Brother Angelo and Brother Joseph, but had a vision of Heaven that stopped them.
___ Two robbers stumbled upon Brother Angelo and Brother Joseph in the woods.
___ Brother Angelo and Brother Joseph told the robbers about Jesus and Mary, and the robbers turned their lives around to be faithful to Christ.
___ Brother Angelo and Brother Joseph were sent on a journey to deliver a letter for Father James.

Activity - Reflection

Discuss with your mom or dad. If you are old enough to write out your response, use the space provided.

Brother Angelo practiced every day to honor Our Lady. When he was young, he made a wreath for her and stayed at her statue to pray. When he got older, he prayed the rosary each day. Do you pray the rosary with your family? Is that something your family could do together?

____

____

____

____

____

Activity - Illustration

Draw a wreath of flowers that you would like to give to Our Lady to show her your love.

Pedro of the Water Jars

Key Terms

These are important people, places, and things you should remember from this story.

Pedro - Young boy who sold water in Palos and joined Christopher Columbus on the Santa Maria on the journey to the New World

Palos - City in Spain where Christopher Columbus and his men departed for their first journey across the Atlantic Ocean.

Don Columbus - Christopher Columbus. Led the first successful expedition to the Americas.

The Pinta, the Nina, and the Santa Maria - Three ships Columbus sailed across the Atlantic Ocean in search of the New World.

Fathers of Saint Francis - Religious order founded by St. Francis of Assisi.

Queen Isabella - Queen of Spain who secured funding for Columbus to sail to the New World.

San Salvador - Island in the Bahamas where Columbus first saw land after the long journey. Name means Holy Savior.

Don - Title given to a royal or nobleman of Spain.

Vocabulary

Read the sentences below and note the use of the word in ***bold****. Write a definition or synonym for this word by considering its context.*

1. I had to fix the two big brown jars on the side of the little **mule**.

2. I had to walk very far outside of Palos to a big **well**.

3. I could hear the waves **beat** against the boat.

4. And there aren't any **queer** people in the water, either.

5. We went to the **palace** of the King and Queen.

Comprehension Questions

To better understand this story, ask yourself these questions and write down your answers using complete sentences.

1. Pedro had a hard time selling water on the first day of the story. Why wasn't he able to sell water that day?

____

____

____

2. The people in the city were sad. Many of the women and children were crying. Why did people feel this way?

____

____

____

3. Why did Pedro dislike the man he called his father?

____

____

____

4. Where did Pedro stop every night before going home? What did he do there?

____

____

5. Pedro came up with a plan. He was excited and hopeful. What was his plan?

____

____

____

6. Why did Pedro go to the church before going to the ships? What did he do at the Church?

____

____

____

7. After Pedro snuck onto the ship, the sailors found him and were very angry. Who came to Pedro's rescue? What job did he offer Pedro?

____

____

____

8. Columbus told Pedro a story about a little boy who was taken from his mother by a bad servant. Pedro told Columbus about the memories he had of a lady with dark eyes and a beautiful smile. What other memories did Pedro have? Why might those memories be important?

____

____

____

9. Columbus and his men sailed back to Palos. Columbus took Pedro to the Palace of the King and Queen. What happened to Pedro when he was at the Palace?

____

____

____

Sequencing

Number the following statements in the same order they occurred in the story.

___ Pedro tried to sell his water in the town but people wouldn't buy it.

___ Columbus cared for Pedro on the ship and told Pedro about the mother who lost her son.

___ Pedro snuck onto the Santa Maria ship and hid.

___ Pedro stopped by the Church on his way home from selling water and had a thought to join the ships Columbus was sailing to the New World.

Number the following statements in the same order they occurred in the story.

___ In Spain, Pedro visited the palace of the King and Queen.

___ After spending some time on land, the voyagers sailed back to Spain.

___ Pedro set eyes on a beautiful lady. She was his mother!

___ The voyagers found land and Columbus named the place San Salvador

Activity - Illustration

Columbus sailed from Palos to the Canary Islands and onward to San Salvador with his fleet of three ships: the Pinta, the Nina, and the Santa Maria. Color the ship below.

Activity - Crossword Puzzle

Complete the crossword puzzle using the vocabulary and key words you found in the text.

Across:

2. The Queen who made it possible for Columbus to sail

5. The sailor who searched for the New World

7. The first land Columbus and his men discovered

Down:

1. The ship that Pedro sailed on during the voyage

3. A title given to a noble or royal man in Spain

4. The animal Pedro used to carry his water jugs

6. The city where the three ships departed from

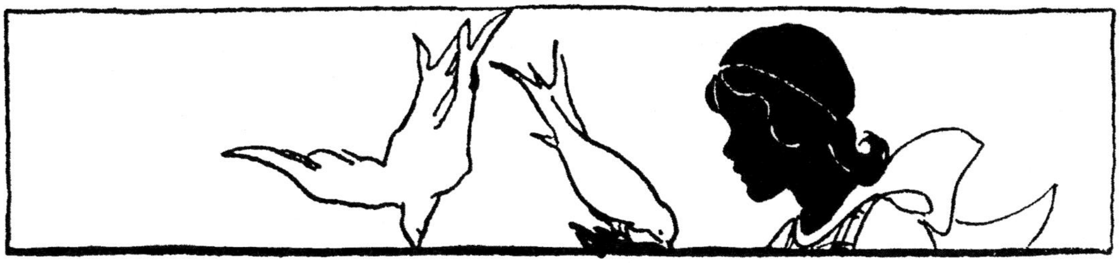

The Little Dove of Our Lady

Key Terms

These are important people, places, and things you should remember from this story.

Zoe - Little girl who lost her mother at a young age. Her sister joined the Sisters of Charity. Canonized St. Catherine Laboure in 1947.

Mary Louise - Zoe's older sister. Joined the Sisters of Charity.

Sisters of Charity - A religious order founded by Saint Vincent de Paul.

Saint Vincent de Paul - A holy saint in Heaven, and the founder of the Sisters of Charity.

Vocabulary

Read the sentences below and note the use of the word in ***bold****. Write a definition or synonym for this word by considering its context.*

1. Mary Louise would let Zoe fill her hands with the **grain** and throw it to the birds.

2. And this wee prayer, like a little white dove with shining wings, flew straight up to Our Lady's heart.

3. Our Lord on the Altar offers Himself to his **Eternal** Father for us.

4. She was **frightened**.

Comprehension Questions

To better understand this story, ask yourself these questions and write down your answers using complete sentences.

1. Zoe and Mary Louise's mother died. Zoe was sad to be without a mother. Who did Mary Louise suggest Zoe take for her mother?

2. After Mary Louise left to join the Sisters of Charity, Zoe continued to go to daily Mass. One night she had a dream. The dream would be very important in her life. What did she see in her dream?

3. What caused Zoe to decide that she wanted to be a Sister of Charity? What did her dream have to do with her decision?

4. Zoe's father did not want her to join the Sisters of Charity. Zoe was devastated. What reason did her father give for telling her "no" the first time she asked?

5. Zoe's father tried hard to keep her from joining the Sisters of Charity. He sent her to Paris, and when that didn't work, he sent her to a big school. He wanted her to forget about becoming a Sister. Zoe finally convinced him! What did she tell him to change his mind?

Sequencing

Number the following statements in the same order they occurred in the story.

___ Mary Louise suggested that Zoe ask the Blessed Mother to take the place of her Mother.

___ After Mass, Mary Louise shared her secret with Zoe. She planned to join the Sisters of Charity and serve the poor.

___ Zoe and Mary Louise's mother became very ill and died.

___ Zoe and Mary Louise spend time together feeding the doves.

___ After some time, Zoe became more cheerful and learned from Mary Louise how to take care of the house.

Number the following statements in the same order they occurred in the story.

___ Zoe realized that her dream about a strange old priest was actually God calling her to join the Sisters of Charity.

___ Finally, Zoe's father was convinced to allow her to join the Sisters of Charity.

___ Zoe had a dream about a strange old priest.

___ Zoe's father sent her to a big school to make her forget about being a Sister.

___ Zoe's father sent her to Paris to make her forget about being a Sister.

Activity - Retelling

See the directions in the Publisher's Preface about how to perform a retelling.

Retell the story in your own words. Think carefully about all the roadblocks Zoe faced on her way to becoming a Sister.

____

____

____

____

____

____

____

____

____

____

The Great Gift of Our Lady

Key Terms

These are important people, places, and things you should remember from this story.

Seminary Sisters - Young girls learning how to be Sisters of Charity.

Sister Catherine - Little Zoe from the story *The Little Dove of Our Lady*. Received the image of the Miraculous Medal in a vision of Our Lady. Canonized St. Catherine Laboure in 1947.

Sister Martha - Taught the little girls to be Sisters of Charity. Instructed them in the care of the poor, the sick, and children.

Father Aladel - First person to hear about the Miraculous Medal from Sister Catherine.

Vocabulary

Read the sentences below and note the use of the word in ***bold****. Write a definition or synonym for this word by considering its context.*

1. God was there in the **Blessed Sacrament.**

2. She was **offering** the world to God.

3. O Mary, conceived without sin, pray for us who have **recourse** to thee.

4. Her Medal is **Miraculous**.

5. But Sister Catherine was not **proud**.

Comprehension Questions

To better understand this story, ask yourself these questions and write down your answers using complete sentences.

1. Sister Martha taught the Seminary Sisters that Our Lady is the Queen of Heaven and of the Saints, and that she is God's Mother. She explained to the girls that Our Lady is also our mother. Sister Catherine thought back to how she felt when her own mother died. She wanted to see Our Lady! Who did Sister Catherine pray to so she could see the Blessed Mother?

2. The second time Sister Catherine saw Our Lady, Mary gave her special directions about the medal Sister Catherine was to have made. Describe the medal that Our Lady asked for.

3. Who did Sister Catherine ask for help to make the Medals? Did this person help her right away?

4. Did Sister Catherine think it was important for people to wear the medal? Why or why not?

5. Why didn't Sister Catherine tell everyone that it was she who saw Our Lady and made the Miraculous Medal?

Sequencing

Number the following statements in the same order they occurred in the story.

___ Sister Catherine prayed to her Guardian Angel and Saint Vincent de Paul to help her see Our Lady.

___ After Sister Catherine saw the Blessed Mother in the Chapel for the first time, she waited and waited to hear what the Blessed Mother wanted her to do.

___ Sister Catherine's Guardian Angel woke her from her sleep and called her to the Chapel.

___ Our Lady told Sister Catherine to make a medal that looked like her so everyone wearing it might receive many graces.

Number the following statements in the same order they occurred in the story.

___ The sisters wore the medals and gave them to the poor and the sick they served.

___ Sister Catherine kept the secret that Our Lady visited her and told her to make the medal for her whole life.

___ Sister Catherine asked Father Aladel to make the medal Mary asked for. He resisted at first, but then had 2,000 medals made.

Activity - Reflection

Discuss with your mom or dad. If you are old enough to write out your response, use the space provided.

Catherine kept the secret of her vision of Our Lady until her death. Only her dear priest friend knew it was she who received the vision of Our Lady. Do you think it was hard for her to keep that secret? Many people came to know Jesus and had miracles because of the medal. Would you want to remain hidden, just like Catherine was? Why or why not?

Activity - Illustration

Color this illustration of Mary.

Black Robe

Key Terms

These are important people, places, and things you should remember from this story.

Father Isaac Jogues - Missionary priest who served the Indian populations in America. Was martyred for the faith. Canonized St. Isaac Jogues in 1930.

Jesuits - Religious order founded by St. Ignatius of Loyola

Rene - Friend of Father Jogues. Doctor who loved children. Martyred by a young Indian. Canonized St. Rene Poupil in 1930.

Mohawk Indians - Violent and dangerous Indian tribe. Hurt other Indians. Killed Rene and Father Jogues. Later produced the first Native American saint, St. Kateri Tekakwitha.

Vocabulary

Read the sentences below and note the use of the word in ***bold****. Write a definition or synonym for this word by considering its context.*

1. These are **wigwams**.

2. They told him how they had taught poor **pagans** about God.

3. Just as he was going in the doorway, one of the Indians hit him on the head with a sharp **hatchet**.

Comprehension Questions

To better understand this story, ask yourself these questions and write down your answers using complete sentences.

1. Mrs. Jogues did not like the Indians. She thought they were very bad people. Isaac had an idea to help the Indians be good people. What was his idea?

2. Why did Isaac want to become a priest?

3. When Father Jogues went to America, did he enjoy living with the Indians?

4. Describe the Mohawk Indians. How did they treat other Indians? How did they treat Father Jogues?

5. Both Rene and Father Jogues were martyred by the Mohawk Indians. The holy men died with one name on their lips. Who did the men cry out to at the moment of death?

Sequencing

Number the following statements in the same order they occurred in the story.

___ Isaac started attending a Jesuit school.
___ Isaac's mother told him that the Indians were bad and in need of a priest.
___ Father Jogues moved to America to live there and minister to the Indians.
___ After learning about all the good work the Jesuit priests do, Isaac decided he wanted to be a priest too.
___ Father Jogues was finally ordained to the priesthood.

Number the following statements in the same order they occurred in the story.

___ Father Jogues escaped his slavery and found his way to New York.
___ Some bad Mohawk Indians hit Father Jogues in the head with a hatchet and killed him. He died with the name of Jesus on his lips.
___ Mohawk Indians captured Father Jogues, cut off his thumb, and made him a slave.
___ Despite his terrible treatment by the Mohawks, Father Jogues returned to America to help the Indians love God.
___ Father Jogues' friend Rene was murdered by a young Indian for showing a child how to pray.
___ Father Jogues was canonized a Saint in Heaven!

Activity - Retelling

See the directions in the Publisher's Preface about how to perform a retelling.

Retell the story in your own words. Think carefully about how hard it was for Father Isaac Jogues to share his faith with the Mohawk Indians. Remember all the things that happened to him after he became a priest.

Catholic Stories for Boys and Girls

Volume 2

Ottawanta

Key Terms

These are important people, places, and things you should remember from this story.

Ottawanta - Indian tribe leader. Followed the teachings of the Black Robes and had his family baptized.

Silver Birch - Ottawanta's wife.

Little Red Bird - Ottawanta's daughter.

Black Robes - Jesuit missionary priests.

Green Snake - Indian leader who refused the teachings of the Black Robes.

Vocabulary

*Read the sentences below and note the use of the word in **bold**. Write a definition or synonym for this word by considering its context.*

1. He was not young, this Indian Chief, nor did he rule over many **braves**.

2. There was a time was when the valley had been filled with noise and **bustle**.

3. Children had played in the stream, and women had sat at the doorways of their wigwams pounding **maize** or weaving bright colored blankets or boiling deer flesh against the return of the braves from the chase or war path.

4. Seven sons tall and strong and **lithe** as young willows had Ottawanta.

5. But Ottawanta and his followers had remained for many peaceful years in the quiet valley, while Green Snake and his band wandered far away to lead a **roving** life in the deeper wilderness.

Comprehension Questions

To better understand this story, ask yourself these questions and write down your answers using complete sentences.

1. Why did Ottawanta's tribe split up?

____

____

____

2. After some time, Ottawanta's tribe members all died. Ottawanta was lonely. He prayed to Our Lady to ease his loneliness. What was his vision?

____

____

____

3. Ottawanta died and he was laid to rest in the grove between his wife and daughter. A shrine was built in this place. What is it called?

____

____

____

Sequencing

Number the following statements in the same order they occurred in the story.

___ Ottawanta's family all died and he was left alone.
___ Ottawanta ruled a busy valley full of Indians.
___ Black Robes came to preach about Christ. Some Indians did not agree. Green Snake led them away.
___ Our Lady promised Ottawanta that a shrine would be built on his land.
___ In prayer, Ottawanta told Our Lady about his loneliness.
___ Ottawanta died and a shrine was built, just as Our Lady said.

Activity - Handwriting

Flower of the Field

Activity - Illustration

The author uses vivid descriptions to create an image of Ottawanta's home. Draw a picture of Ottawanta's home following the descriptions from the book.

"On the banks of the Tomsquit that flowed down the side of Indian Lookout Mountain and crossed the quiet valley below"

"Children had played in the stream"

"climbed the hill to the oak grove"

"there was a great cross"

"fairest flowers of spring"

"brightest leaves and fruits of autumn"

Elizabeth Bayley Seton

Key Terms

These are important people, places, and things you should remember from this story.

Betty Ann - An American born girl who opened schools and hospitals for the poor. Canonized St. Elizabeth Ann Seton in 1975.

Mistress Hannah - Betty's nanny and teacher.

Doctor Bayley - Betty's father. Supported the Americans in their fight for freedom against the British.

General George Washington - Commander of the United States armed forces. Friend of the Bayley family.

Marquis de LaFayette - French general who helped America in the Revolutionary War. Friend of the Bayley family.

Vocabulary

*Read the sentences below and note the use of the word in **bold**. Write a definition or synonym for this word by considering its context.*

1. Yes, it was a pretty **sampler**.

2. They have not been treated **justly**, Betty.

3. Father wishes his little daughter to know how to play the **spinet** and speak French.

4. Betty **curtsied** to the very floor when he spoke to her.

5. Betty looked up and saw the **courtly** gentleman in white satin and her father standing by the spinet.

Comprehension Questions

To better understand this story, ask yourself these questions and write down your answers using complete sentences.

1. Betty's father supported the Americans in their fight against the British. How did Doctor Bayley feel about the Americans?

____

____

2. Doctor Bayley recommended Betty change the name of her dolls. What did he suggest she call them?

____

____

3. Betty's father took her on a long journey. Where did they go? Who did they visit?

____

____

____

4. Betty's father taught her a very important lesson. What was that lesson?

____

____

____

5. Betty grew. She married and went by the name Elizabeth. After Elizabeth's husband died, she wanted to become a Sister. She founded the Sisters of Charity in the United States. Were things very easy for her and her new order? Why or why not?

____

____

____

6. Elizabeth died. Did the Sisters of Charity continue doing God's work after she passed away?

____

____

____

Sequencing

Number the following statements in the same order they occurred in the story.

___ Betty gave her dolls new names.

___ On a trip to Mount Vernon, Betty spoke French with Marquis de LaFayette and played spinet for General Washington and his guests.

___ Doctor Bayley taught Betty about the good works the Americans were doing in their fight for freedom.

___ American troops finally made it to New York City. The English flag was torn down from the flagpole and replaced with the American flag.

___ Betty was naughty and gave Mistress Hannah trouble because she didn't want to use books written anywhere but in America.

Number the following statements in the same order they occurred in the story.

___ After Mother Seton died, the Sisters opened many schools and hospitals all across the country.

___ Betty grew older and now went by the name Elizabeth Ann. She married and had five children.

___ Elizabeth founded the Sisters of Charity in the United States. Their land was in the same place that Chief Ottawanta had lived and died.

___ After Elizabeth's husband died, she received the holy gift of Faith. She wanted to become a Catholic.

Activity - Reflection

Discuss with your mom or dad. If you are old enough to write out your response, use the space provided.

Elizabeth made many big and little sacrifices in her life to serve God. She even drank coffee made from carrots! What is one little sacrifice you can do today or this week to serve God?

____

____

____

Activity - Retelling

See the directions in the Publisher's Preface about how to perform a retelling.

Retell the story in your own words. Think carefully about Elizabeth's life, and especially about the lasting impact she made on the lives of the poor and sick.

Anina

Key Terms

These are important people, places, and things you should remember from this story.

Anina - One of Elizabeth Ann Seton's little daughters. Grew up to join the Sisters of Charity.
Ma - Elizabeth Ann Seton, or little Betty Ann. Anina's mother.
Pa - William M. Seton. Anina's father.

Vocabulary

Read the sentences below and note the use of the word in ***bold****. Write a definition or synonym for this word by considering its context.*

1. Anina had finished the New England **Primer** clear through.

2. Sometimes Anina could see the great waves **dashing** against the rocks.

3. When the ship reached Italy, the people thought that Anina, her father, and mother had **yellow fever**.

4. They made them go to a strange kind of a house built near the shore. It was called a **Lazaretto**.

5. They were in **quarantine**.

6. There were ten in each band or **decury**.

7. She received **Holy Viaticum** and Extreme Unction.

Comprehension Questions

To better understand this story, ask yourself these questions and write down your answers using complete sentences.

1. When Elizabeth Ann Seton was a child, her baby sister Kitty died. Elizabeth didn't cry at her funeral. Why not?

____

____

____

2. What gift did Ma give to Anina for her sixth birthday?

____

____

____

3. Anina and Ma had a discussion about the Kingdom of God. Anina was having trouble understanding the idea of eternity. What were some of the ways Ma helped her understand it?

____

____

____

4. Why did the Seton family have to stay in the Lazaretto?

____

____

____

5. Anina's favorite word was 'eternity.' Why do you think that was?

____

____

Sequencing

Number the following statements in the same order they occurred in the story.

___ When Anina was six years old, she spent the summer with her family at the seashore.
___ Anina's father got even sicker and died.
___ Anina and her parents were put in quarantine for a month in the Lazaretto before being allowed to leave and travel to Italy.
___ Anina traveled across the Atlantic to Italy on a ship in hopes that her father could be healed from his illness.

Number the following statements in the same order they occurred in the story.

___ Anina and her mother were received into the Catholic Church.
___ Anina became sick and died. The last words on her mouth were, "Laugh, mother, Jesus."
___ As the Seton family prepared to come home to America, Anina became sick with scarlet fever.
___ Anina joined the Sisters of Charity as a novice and became a teacher.

Activity - Retelling

See the directions in the Publisher's Preface about how to perform a retelling.

Retell the story in your own words.

____

____

____

____

____

____

____

____

____

____

____

____

____

____

Activity - Illustration

Color the word 'Eternity' below. Use illustrations that make you think about living forever with God in Heaven.

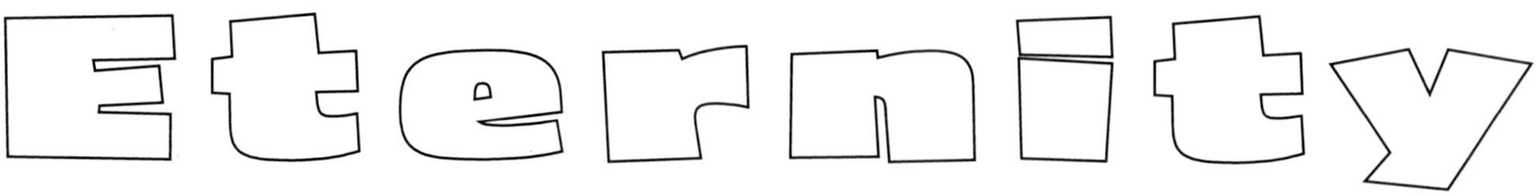

Silver Wings

Key Terms

These are important people, places, and things you should remember from this story.

Mary Gertrude - A young girl who moved to St. Joseph's Boarding School.

Silver Wings - Small airplane flown by Mary Gertrude's Father.

Miss Keenan - Mother's nurse and caretaker.

St. Joseph's - Boarding school Mary Gertrude and her mother both attended. Located in Maryland.

Pandora - A tame squirrel that ate nuts out of Mary Gertrude's hands.

Father Deaver - Franciscan Friar who died on the road while taking the Blessed Sacrament to a sick woman.

Vocabulary

Read the sentences below and note the use of the word in ***bold****. Write a definition or synonym for this word by considering its context.*

1. Lessons and games and long **corridors** and little girls like herself.

2. In a minute Mary Gertrude was out the door and down the staircase to the long corridor that led to the **parlors**.

3. April came and Mary Gertrude **reveled** in the beautiful sights that spring brought to St. Joseph's Valley.

4. There have been beautiful people in **spangled** clothes, and music and clowns and animals.

5. Her **trunks** could be packed and sent later.

Comprehension Questions

To better understand this story, ask yourself these questions and write down your answers using complete sentences.

1. Why did Mary Gertrude need to go to St. Joseph's?

____

____

2. Why did Mary Gertrude want to attend Mass every day?

____

____

3. When Mary Gertrude felt afraid while she was flying on Silver Wings, what did she do to calm her fears?

____

____

____

4. Did the trip in Silver Wings go quickly? Why or why not?

____

____

____

5. When Daddy was flying through the Rocky Mountains, Mary Gertrude saw something that caused her alarm. She asked Daddy to land the plane. What did she see?

____

____

____

Sequencing

Number the following statements in the same order they occurred in the story.

___ Mary Gertrude's father visited her from New York. He brought gifts and promised Mary Gertrude to take her on Silver Wings if she was obedient and studied well.

___ Mary Gertrude's mother was unwell. She needed to go to California and was unable to care for Mary Gertrude.

___ June finally came, and Mary Gertrude received her First Holy Communion.

___ Mary Gertrude traveled with her father on the train to St. Joseph's Boarding School in Maryland.

Number the following statements in the same order they occurred in the story.

___ After the Friar died, Mary Gertrude was tasked with carrying the Blessed Sacrament back to California.

___ Mary Gertrude and Daddy arrived in California. They finally met Mother again and Mary Gertrude's new baby brother!

___ Daddy arrived at St. Joseph's to pick up Mary Gertrude and take her to California in Silver Wings.

___ On Mary Gertrude and Daddy's trip back to California in Silver Wings, they stopped to help an old Franciscan Friar who was lying in the road.

Activity - Word Search

The following is an optional activity used to help your comprehension of the text. Answer the questions from Silver Wings *and locate the answers in the word search on the following page. Note: the words also appear horizontally.*

1. ______________ attended St. Joseph's Boarding School when she had no one in her family to care for her.
2. After she received her First Holy ____________, it was important for Mary Gertrude to go to _______ every day.
3. Mary Gertrude saw a _________________ Friar lying in the road on her flight back to _______________.
4. The trip in ____________ took many days, and Mary Gertrude and her father had to stop and sleep in hotels at night.
5. The old Franciscan _______ died, but Mary Gertrude took the _________ with her all the way to California.

K	B	O	K	C	N	M	T	F	H	M	R	W	E	S
Z	Z	M	S	Z	A	Y	P	D	O	A	E	K	U	I
H	P	Y	P	A	V	L	D	W	M	R	V	G	C	L
B	D	A	R	L	R	Z	I	M	Y	Y	Z	X	H	V
K	F	N	E	C	Z	D	F	F	V	G	J	H	A	E
H	C	R	J	E	Z	Z	R	Y	O	E	O	V	R	R
P	X	O	A	G	E	T	I	J	J	R	U	M	I	W
N	P	O	M	N	S	I	A	L	V	T	N	P	S	I
X	T	M	O	M	C	K	R	I	Q	R	M	I	T	N
F	H	M	V	E	U	I	I	Q	A	U	F	N	A	G
X	J	E	X	L	X	N	S	C	D	D	J	R	U	S
T	D	H	Z	U	M	X	I	C	S	E	F	A	H	M
I	A	K	G	C	S	W	C	O	A	W	E	P	Z	O
O	Q	J	H	X	G	N	P	K	N	N	P	K	A	T
M	A	S	S	G	I	T	P	H	G	R	D	G	X	Q

California
Friar
Communion

Eucharist
Franciscan
Silver Wings

Mass
Gertrude

Activity - Reflection

Discuss with your mom or dad. If you are old enough to write out your response, use the space provided.

Have you received your First Holy Communion yet? When will you receive your First Holy Communion if you haven't already? Mary Gertrude went to Mass every day after she received her First Holy Communion. How will you make Mass an important part of your life?

John Philip

Key Terms

These are important people, places, and things you should remember from this story.

John Philip - Loved to fish. Wanted to go to the circus. Thought about being a priest like Father Lambert when he grew up.

Aunt Hannah - Planned to help watch the Briggs children so John Philip could attend the circus.

Mrs. Briggs - Neighbor that attended Mass with John Philip's mother. Mother of three young children.

Uncle Bernard - John Philip's rich uncle from Syracuse. Took John Philip on an adventure.

Father Lambert - Priest at John Philip's parish. Young and holy. Played baseball and told funny stories.

Our Lady's Assumption - Mary was taken body and soul into Heaven. Celebrated on August 15.

The Lake - Lake Ontario

Vocabulary

*Read the sentences below and note the use of the word in **bold**. Write a definition or synonym for this word by considering its context.*

1. And John Philip would wear his red **cassock** and white **surplice**.

2. He said his **penance** in front of Our Lady's statue.

Comprehension Questions

To better understand this story, ask yourself these questions and write down your answers using complete sentences.

1. John Philip had been looking forward to going to the circus. Mother told him the plans had changed. What happened to cause John Philip to miss the circus?

____

____

____

____

2. Uncle Bernard took John Philip on a long journey. John Philip was so surprised and happy. Where did Uncle Bernard take John Philip?

____

____

____

____

3. What game did John Philip play with the Briggs children when their mother was away at Mass?

____

____

____

Sequencing

Number the following statements in the same order they occurred in the story.

___ Uncle Bernard and John Philip arrived at the hotel and had a wonderful breakfast while watching the circus parade go by on the street.

___ Uncle Bernard woke John Philip to let him know they would go for a ride the next morning.

___ After John Philip finished his morning chores and his breakfast, he went fishing.

___ Mother broke the bad news that Aunt Hannah would not be able to watch the Briggs children, and John Philip would have to miss the circus after all.

Number the following statements in the same order they occurred in the story.

___ John Philip served at Mass on the Solemnity of the Assumption.
___ John Philip and Uncle Bernard went to the Lake to swim and play.
___ John Philip went to the Briggs' home to watch the children. They played circus.
___ Uncle Bernard and John Philip went to the circus. John Philip was overjoyed!

Activity - Reflection

Discuss with your mom or dad. If you are old enough to write out your response, use the space provided.

Father Lambert says, "The more we do for the Blessed Mother, the more she does for us." What can you do for the Blessed Mother to show her your love?

Activity - Illustration

Color the circus tent. Inside the tent, color a picture of your favorite circus animal.

Catholic Stories for Boys and Girls

Volume 3

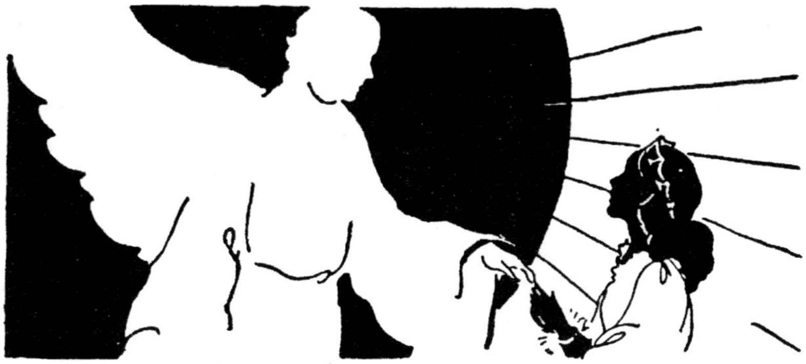

Begga's Bracelet

Key Terms

These are important people, places, and things you should remember from this story.

Begga - Princess who didn't want to marry. Escaped to live a life for God.

Prince of Norway - Brave, rich, and young. Engaged to be married to Begga.

Vocabulary

*Read the sentences below and note the use of the word in **bold**. Write a definition or synonym for this word by considering its context.*

1. You are God's little **lily**.

2. She promised that she would always try to **please** God.

Comprehension Questions

To better understand this story, ask yourself these questions and write down your answers using complete sentences.

1. During Begga's first encounter with her Guardian Angel, what did the Angel tell her?

___

___

___

2. What did Begga's Guardian Angel give her?

___

___

___

3. Why did Begga not want to marry?

___

___

___

___

4. How did Begga escape the castle?

___

___

___

___

5. Did Begga's father ever forgive her for leaving him?

___

___

___

___

Sequencing

Number the following statements in the same order they occurred in the story.

___ Begga grew older. Many suitors came to try to marry Begga. She did not want to marry.
___ Begga saw her Guardian Angel in the Chapel. The Angel gave her a bracelet.
___ Begga spent her time learning, playing, and praying. She loved to visit the Chapel.
___ Begga's mother called Begga in to tell her she was dying. She told Begga to ask her Guardian Angel for help and to keep her soul white like a lily.
___ A kind fisherman took care of Begga and built her a house. Soon girls followed Begga so they could serve the poor too.
___ The King wanted Begga to marry the Prince of Norway.
___ Begga's Guardian Angel helped her escape to a foreign land.

Activity - Retelling

See the directions in the Publisher's Preface about how to perform a retelling.

Retell the story in your own words.

____

____

____

____

____

____

____

____

____

____

____

____

____

____

Activity - True/False

Read each question carefully. If the answer is true, circle true. If the answer is false, circle false.

1. For Begga's whole life, she hoped to marry a prince. True/False
2. Begga saw her Guardian Angel in a vision. True/False
3. Begga's Guardian Angel gave her a necklace. True/False
4. Begga's father died when she was a young child. True/False
5. A kind fisherman built a house for Begga to live in. True/False
6. Begga was a good example to other girls to help them serve the poor. True/False

In the Tower of London

Key Terms

These are important people, places, and things you should remember from this story.

Queen Elizabeth - Wicked Queen of England who hated Catholics.

Father Edmund Campion - Holy priest. Would not deny the teachings of the Catholic Church. Was martyred for his faith. Canonized St. Edmund Campion in 1970.

Richard of Blainscow - A good Catholic. Father of 12 sons.

Robert, Richard, Thomas, and John - The Blainscow sons who hoped to become priests. Were captured and held by the Queen's men before being freed by their father.

Father Thomas - Blainscow boys' uncle. A priest in France.

False Bishop Chatterton - Former Catholic. Worked for the wicked Queen Elizabeth.

Vocabulary

Read the sentences below and note the use of the word in ***bold****. Write a definition or synonym for this word by considering its context.*

1. They used to make themselves look like **merchants** or servants.

2. They would go through the country **disguised**.

3. Father Campion had been saved by a **quick-witted** servant girl.

4. He looked fearlessly at the **gallows**, the sharp knives, and the black bubbling **pitch**, beneath the tree nearby.

Comprehension Questions

To better understand this story, ask yourself these questions and write down your answers using complete sentences.

1. When the Queen's men were looking for Father Campion at the Blainscow home, a little servant girl acted quickly to save Father Edmund. What did she do?

2. When the Queen's men finally found Father Campion, where did they lock him up?

3. The false bishop sent men to do many bad things to Richard, Robert, Thomas, and John. What did the bad men do?

4. How was Richard of Blainscow able to rescue his sons from imprisonment?

5. What happened to the four Blainscow boys after they escaped to France?

Sequencing

Number the following statements in the same order they occurred in the story.

___ Eventually, Father Edmund Campion was found by the Queen's men and locked away in the Tower of London.

___ The Queen's men came to take away Father Campion and a little servant girl pushed him into the pond. He escaped capture that day.

___ Queen Elizabeth had Father Campion killed because he would not deny his Catholicism.

___ The wicked Queen Elizabeth hated Catholics and wanted to stop the Catholic Church in England.

Number the following statements in the same order they occurred in the story.

___ Father Thomas was kept in the Tower of London for a long time. He was eventually able to return to France.

___ Father Thomas came to take some of the Blainscow boys back to France. They were captured on their way by the Queen's men.

___ Richard of Blainscow heard of his sons' imprisonment and journeyed to find them. He freed them and they fled to France.

___ The false Bishop of Chatterton tried to convince the boys to give up their faith time after time. The boys refused to give up their faith.

Activity - Reflection

Discuss with your mom or dad. If you are old enough to write out your response, use the space provided.

Catholics suffered a great deal when wicked Queen Elizabeth ruled England. The Blainscow boys were just children and they went through many difficult struggles at the hands of the false Bishop of Chatterton. When they were told to stop being Catholic, they were brave and never gave up. Could you keep your faith, even when things were so hard? Do you think you could be brave like the Blainscow boys? Why or why not? This week, ask Jesus to help you be a strong Catholic.

____

____

____

____

____

____

Activity - Crossword Puzzle

Complete the crossword puzzle using the vocabulary and key words you found in the text.

Across:

4. Wicked Queen of England

5. Father of 12 sons

6. Country where Fr. Thomas and the Blainscow boys fled after their captivity

Down:

1. Holy Catholic priest who became a saint

2. Place where Fr. Edmund Campion was locked up

3. Structure used to hang people

Joseph

Key Terms

These are important people, places, and things you should remember from this story.

Joseph - A shepherd boy. Grew up to be St. Joseph, foster father to Jesus.

Mary - Mother of Jesus. Joseph's wife.

Vocabulary

*Read the sentences below and note the use of the word in **bold**. Write a definition or synonym for this word by considering its context.*

1. He stood up quickly and held his big shepherd's **staff** tightly.

2. He ran over to where the wolf was and struck it again and again with the blazing **bough**.

3. Joseph had become a **carpenter.**

Comprehension Questions

To better understand this story, ask yourself these questions and write down your answers using complete sentences.

1. Why were the lambs safer when the fire was burning?

2. How did the little girl escape from her captors?

3. The girl was safe with Joseph's family. Where did she go when she left his home?

4. Joseph had a vision. The voice in the vision told him he had to protect someone. Who was Joseph going to protect?

5. When Joseph was older, he was called to the Temple. A young woman was there because it was time for her to be married. The young woman knew right away that Joseph was the right one to wed. How did she know?

6. How did Joseph know to take Mary and baby Jesus away to Egypt to save Him from the wicked King Herod?

7. When it was time for Joseph to die, was he afraid or sad?

Sequencing

Number the following statements in the same order they occurred in the story.

___ Joseph, a young shepherd, was tending the flock in the field.

___ Joseph had a dream about the young girl praying in the Temple of Jerusalem.

___ A young girl ran through his field, desperate to hide from bad men who kidnapped her from her family.

___ Joseph grew older and became a carpenter. He was called to the Temple because a woman was there who needed a husband.

___ Joseph hid the girl from the bad men among the lambs and kept her safe until her father came to take her home.

Number the following statements in the same order they occurred in the story.

___ Joseph took his family to Egypt so Herod could not kill Jesus.

___ Mary and Joseph were married. Jesus was born.

___ The woman in the temple was the same woman from Joseph's dream! Joseph was chosen!

___ The Holy Family returned to their home and lived a happy life until Joseph died.

Activity - Handwriting

Trace the following sentence.

Activity - Retelling

See the directions in the Publisher's Preface about how to perform a retelling.

Retell the story in your own words.

Louise

Key Terms

These are important people, places, and things you should remember from this story.

Anton - Marillac family cook. Cared for Armand.

Lady Louise de Marillac - Wealthy child. Served the poor. Canonized St. Louise de Marillac in 1934.

Armand - Poor chimney sweep. Worked in the Marillac family home with Anton.

Mr. Marillac - Louise's father. Took her to see the poor and allowed her to serve them.

Marguerite Nasseau - Woman sent by St. Vincent to help serve the poor with Louise.

St. Vincent de Paul - Founded the Sisters of Charity.

Vocabulary

Read the sentences below and note the use of the word in ***bold****. Write a definition or synonym for this word by considering its context.*

1. The **chimney sweep** fell on his knees and put his dirty hands on her knee.

2. He looked at her pretty blue silk night dress, **trimmed** with lovely lace.

3. The driver, in blue and gold, cracked his long whip over the backs of the horses and away they went.

4. One day there was a big **rap** on the kitchen door and the tall man walked in.

5. A terrible **plague** broke out in France just at this time.

Comprehension Questions

To better understand this story, ask yourself these questions and write down your answers using complete sentences.

1. Lady Louise loved the treats Anton baked for her. Anton was happy to work for her family and knew just what she would like because he had a little daughter of his own. When Louise first called Anton in to speak to him, she gave him something. What did she put in his hand?

2. Louise asked her father to take her to see the poor. What were some of the things they saw on the ride through town?

3. From that point on, Louise knew she wanted to serve the poor. Did her father allow her to serve the poor? Did she continue serving the poor when she grew up?

4. When Louise went to villages to serve the poor, she did more than just serve the poor. She also taught the people in the village. What did she teach them?

5. How did Marguerite learn to read?

6. What were some of the things the Sisters of Charity did in service to the poor?

Sequencing

Number the following statements in the same order they occurred in the story.

___ Mr. Marillac took Louise to a poor neighborhood. She felt sad to see how other people lived.

___ The bad man came back for the chimney sweep. Little did he know it was Armand, safe and sound.

___ She entrusted the chimney sweep to the care of Anton in the kitchen.

___ Louise was awakened in the night when a chimney sweep boy climbed out of her fireplace.

Number the following statements in the same order they occurred in the story

___ Marguerite joined Louise in serving the poor, but soon died from the plague.

___ Louise grew up and married. She had a son, and then her husband died.

___ Louise prayed when a poor child had been run over. The child survived! It was a miracle.

___ St. Vincent helped Louise after her husband died.

Activity - Reflection

Discuss with your mom or dad. If you are old enough to write out your response, use the space provided.

Louise thought it was so important to serve the poor. What is one way you can serve the poor this week? Maybe you could give away one of your toys to a child with no toys, or go to the store to buy food to take to a food pantry.

Activity - Illustration

Illustrate the picture below of this act of service: feeding the poor.

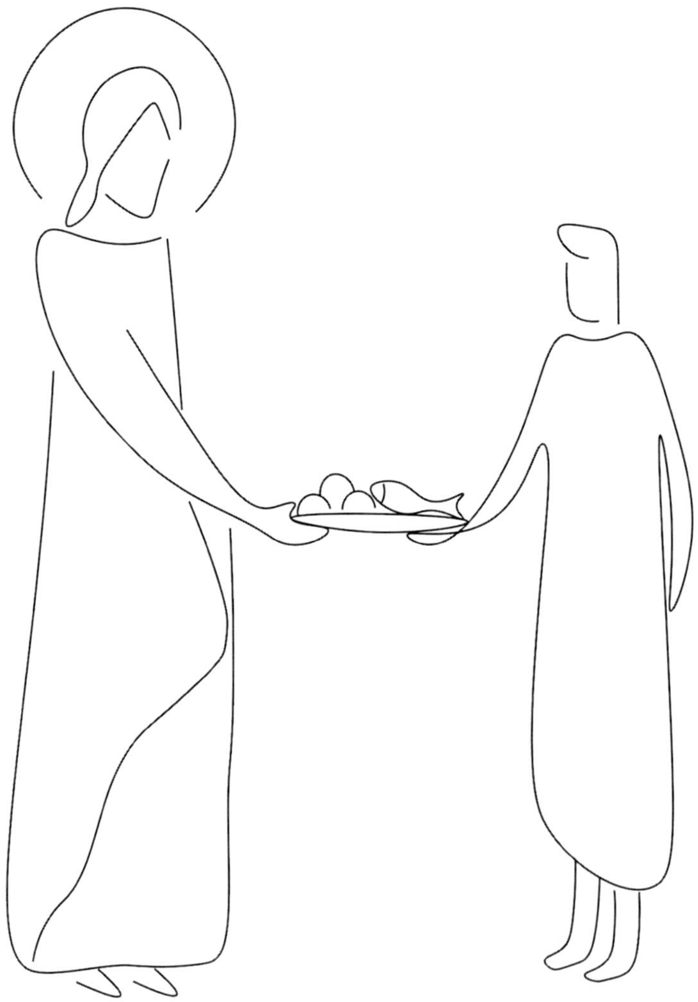

Catholic Stories for Boys and Girls

Volume 4

The Dawn of Spring

Key Terms

These are important people, places, and things you should remember from this story.

Old Louis - An old toymaker. Lived with his daughter and her family.

Marguerite, little Louis, and Jean - Old Louis' grandchildren.

Vocabulary

Read the sentences below and note the use of the word in ***bold****. Write a definition or synonym for this word by considering its context.*

1. Old Louis was a **cripple**.

2. Old Louis knew the little **brook** well.

3. The mountainside was **gilded** with sunshine.

Comprehension Questions

To better understand this story, ask yourself these questions and write down your answers using complete sentences.

1. Old Louis told the children stories of his youth. He heard the children play. He became sad. Why did Louis feel sad?

2. Old Louis had a vision of the forest. What did it look like?

3. Old Louis saw silvery mist and felt a soft wind touch his cheek. The mist wasn't mist at all, but the wings of angels. How did the angels change the forest?

4. Old Louis saw a boy in his vision. Who was the boy, and what did the boy tell him?

5. Marguerite thought Louis said spring would return in a few days, but he wasn't talking about the return of spring. What did he mean?

Sequencing

Number the following statements in the same order they occurred in the story.

___ Louis had a vision of angels and a little boy in the forest.
___ Old Louis thought all about how sad he was to be getting older.
___ Louis found happiness again and was ready to go to Heaven.
___ The grandchildren asked Louis to tell them a story and he declined.

Activity - Word Search

The following is an optional activity used to help your comprehension of the text. Answer the questions from The Dawn of Spring *and locate the answers in the word search. Note: the words also appear horizontally.*

1. Old Louis had three young ____________ that he loved to tell stories to.
2. After Old Louis had a _______ of the angels, he longed to go to ________.
3. Old Louis's young grandchildren were called_____________, _____________, and young ____________ .
4. Old Louis couldn't walk well because he was a __________.
5. The __________ thawed the forest so spring would come.

J W N V Q R K S R S A M L E Y
U M G I B P I P L L F V X U J
X Z F A V Q P E K D O I X I K
Y B I S D N G U W Q J U T F M
U U E J A N L F B X K H I S A
M L X E A M V B J Y Q J W S R
B A A A A B Q W V E J D B V G
G R A N D C H I L D R E N I U
E Y J D Q G I B P N M A W S E
V F Q U Y H X U K P E W M I R
Q J S E G G R W S R Z V P O I
C R I P P L E Y S C B C A N T
A T U X F M C I R U H U A E E
D G G X W L Y N L X E V D J H
E Z S H W G O U F H G T M X D

Jean	Louis	Heaven	Marguerite
Vision	Cripple	Grandchildren	Angels

Activity - Retelling

See the directions in the Publisher's Preface about how to perform a retelling.

Retell the story in your own words.

The Land of Erin

Key Terms

These are important people, places, and things you should remember from this story.

Patrick - Saint Patrick. Nephew to St. Martin of Tours.
Erin - Another name for Ireland. God chose to save Erin.
Margot - Patrick's sister. Was healed by God.
Milcho - Bad and very mean man who bought Patrick and kept him as a slave.
Conchessa - Patrick's mother.
Odran - Drove Patrick's horses in Erin. Changed places with Patrick and died in his place.

Vocabulary

*Read the sentences below and note the use of the word in **bold**. Write a definition or synonym for this word by considering its context.*

1. The heart of Bishop Patrick went up, up, up, to the skies with the little red lark, in gladness.

2. We shall light the blessed fire on **Holy Saturday** as Mother Church tells us.

3. He picked a little clover, or as the people of Erin would say, a **shamrock**.

4. She brought him a beautiful **cloak**.

Comprehension Questions

To better understand this story, ask yourself these questions and write down your answers using complete sentences.

1. The people of Erin were strong, brave, and beautiful. They were good. They didn't steal and they told the truth. But something about them made God feel sorry for them. Why did God feel sorry for the people in Erin?

____

____

____

2. Patrick heard a voice one day while he was praying. What did the voice tell him? What did Patrick do?

____

____

____

3. Why did the Pope want Patrick to return to Erin after he became a priest?

____

____

____

4. Patrick went against the King and lit his fire on Holy Saturday. The pagan priests were angry. How did the pagan priest die?

____

____

____

5. Did Patrick baptize the King's daughters right away? Why or why not? When they were baptized, what did Patrick name them?

____

____

____

Sequencing

Number the following statements in the same order they occurred in the story.

___ Patrick's Guardian Angel led him to a ship, and Patrick sailed home to his family.
___ Patrick's sister, Margot, fell and cut her head, and she was healed when Patrick prayed to God for her healing.
___ Patrick worked for six long years as a slave for Milcho.
___ Pirates captured Patrick and took him to be a slave in the land of Erin.

Number the following statements in the same order they occurred in the story.

___ Patrick studied and became a priest and, later, a bishop.
___ Patrick showed the pagan priests that God is all powerful.
___ The Pope gave Patrick permission to return to Erin and be a missionary.
___ When Patrick was over 100 years old, he finally died, and his soul was taken to Heaven.

Activity - Retelling

See the directions in the Publisher's Preface about how to perform a retelling.

Retell the story in your own words.

The Flowery Kingdom

Key Terms

These are important people, places, and things you should remember from this story.

Louis - John Gabriel's brother who became Father Louis Perboryre.
Basil - Boy that stole the pocketbook.
John Gabriel - Louis' brother who became Father John Gabriel Perboyre. Canonized Saint John Gabriel Perboyre.
Father Perboyre - Louis and John Gabriel's uncle.
Flowery Kingdom - Father Perboyre's name for the country of China.
Mandarin - A kind of leader in China.
Kowtow - A type of pagan bowing the Chinese do.
Father Francis Regis Clet - A Vincentian missionary in China. Died for his faith.

Vocabulary

Read the sentences below and note the use of the word in **bold**. *Write a definition or synonym for this word by considering its context.*

1. There was a **rap** at the door.

2. First came a number of old **stockings**.

3. He sent his servants for a kind of bed called a **litter**.

Comprehension Questions

To better understand this story, ask yourself these questions and write down your answers using complete sentences.

1. Why did John Gabriel fight Basil?

___

___

___

2. When John Gabriel was finally away at school to become a priest, how did he serve the poor?

___

___

___

3. John Gabriel became a priest. He wanted to leave right away to go to China. Why wasn't he allowed to go?

___

___

___

4. Father John Gabriel was caught by the Mandarin. The Mandarin treated Father John Gabriel very poorly. What did the Mandarin want Father John Gabriel to do?

___

___

___

5. Father John Gabriel was martyred. What happened in the sky after he was killed?

___

___

___

Sequencing

Number the following statements in the correct order they occurred in the story.

___ John Gabriel taught the children a new game about Mandarins and Vincentians.
___ Basil stole the pocketbook and after being caught, apologized.
___ John Gabriel taught all the children about the Chinese.
___ After a long time waiting, Father John Gabriel went to China.
___ John Gabriel studied and finally became a priest.
___ Father John Gabriel was captured, tortured, and eventually killed.

Activity - True/False

Read each question carefully. If the answer is true, circle true. If the answer is false, circle false.

1. Louis stole the pocketbook from his teacher and blamed Basil. True/False
2. John Gabriel taught his classmates about the Chinese. True/False
3. John Gabriel never wanted to play games. True/False
4. When John Gabriel became a priest, he went to China right away. True/False
5. Father John Gabriel was caught by the Mandarin. True/False
6. Father John Gabriel kept his faith and never turned his back on Jesus. True/False

Activity - Reflection

Discuss with your mom or dad. If you are old enough to write out your response, use the space provided.

It must have been very difficult for Father John Gabriel to stay true to his faith. The Mandarin wanted him to step on a cross, and he could have been freed! If Father John Gabriel did what the Mandarin asked him, he would not have been killed. Could you be brave like that? Would you have been scared? This week, pray to God to help you be strong and brave in your faith.

____

____

____

____

____

____

The Lion Tamer

Key Terms

These are important people, places, and things you should remember from this story.

Martina - Would not marry Emperor Alexander. Stayed true to the faith.

Emperor Alexander - Roman leader. Believed in false idols.

Vocabulary

Read the sentences below and note the use of the word in ***bold****. Write a definition or synonym for this word by considering its context.*

1. Did you never wonder why we have to go away down underneath the ground in the **Catacombs** to hear Holy Mass?

2. They worship false **idols**.

3. A **fierce** wind came and blew the fire away from her.

Comprehension Questions

To better understand this story, ask yourself these questions and write down your answers using complete sentences.

1. Why did Martina, her family, and the other Christians have to be quiet and hide when they attended Mass?

2. Why were there circus animals marching through Rome?

3. Martina's mother wanted her to have many rich jewels. Martina did not want to keep them. What did Martina wish for her mother to do instead?

4. How was Martina caught and put into prison?

5. Why did Emperor Alexander have Martina whipped and beat? What happened during the beating?

6. What were some other ways the Emperor tried to have Martina killed? How was she killed?

Sequencing

Number the following statements in the same order they occurred in the story.

___ Emperor Alexander wanted to marry Martina, but only if she would stop being a Christian.
___ Martina prayed to God to break the idol of Apollo, and the idol was destroyed.
___ Martina's mother told her why the wild circus animals were brought to Rome.
___ Martina did not want to keep her mother's jewels.

Number the following statements in the same order they occurred in the story.

___ Guards beat and whipped Martina, but she was saved from death.
___ The Emperor tried to burn her, but she did not die.
___ Emperor Alexander was so upset that Martina would not give up her faith that he had her head cut off.
___ Martina was sent to the lions but they didn't eat her.
___ Martina was locked in the Temple of Jupiter, and God destroyed the idol.

Activity - Crossword Puzzle

Complete the crossword puzzle using the vocabulary and key words you found in the text.

Across:

2. False god whose idol Martina asked God to destroy

3. Underground cemeteries cemetery connected by tunnels

4. Image of a false god used for worship

6. A roman leader

Down:

1. Name of the emperor who wanted to marry Martina

5. Animals that were supposed to eat Martina

A Shepherd and His Sheep

Key Terms

These are important people, places, and things you should remember from this story.

Vincent - Shepherd boy who became a priest. Canonized St. Vincent de Paul in 1737.
Pierre - Vincent's dog.
Turks - Turkish pirates.
Lady Marguerite - Mother of a rich and noble family. Father Vincent lived with her family. Lord Philip's wife.
Lord Philip - Father of a rich and noble family. Head of the prisons. Lady Marguerite's husband.
Priests of the Mission - Priests who followed St. Vincent, also known as Vincentians.
King Louis - French king who asked Father Vincent to take care of all the prisoners in France.

Vocabulary

Read the sentences below and note the use of the word in ***bold****. Write a definition or synonym for this word by considering its context.*

1. One beautiful morning in September he was **ordained**.

2. These ships were called **galleys.**

Comprehension Questions

To better understand this story, ask yourself these questions and write down your answers using complete sentences.

1. Vincent's parents taught their children that riches wouldn't make them happy. What did his mother and father say would make them happy?

2. At the beginning of the story, Vincent had three dollars. He wanted to use it to go to school to become a priest. Where did his money go?

3. How did Father Vincent leave the life of slavery?

4. Father Vincent saw an old man before he died. The man was afraid to go to confession. Why was he scared? How did Father Vincent help him?

5. Father Vincent went to Paris. He saw many things that made him sad. List some of the things that made Father Vincent sad.

6. Father Vincent was taken as a galley slave. How did this happen?

____

____

____

7. Father Vincent was almost killed by robbers! They thought he was carrying treasure. He was carrying treasure, but not the kind they wanted. What did Father Vincent tell the robbers?

____

____

____

Sequencing

Number the following statements in the same order they occurred in the story.

___ Vincent gave the sad woman all of the money he was saving for school to become a priest.

___ Father Vincent returned to his home country of France with one of his slave owners and the slave owner's wife.

___ Vincent's father saved up enough money and Vincent was able to go to school to become a priest.

___ After Vincent became a priest, he started on a long journey. He was captured by pirates!

Number the following statements in the same order they occurred in the story.

___ Father Vincent moved to Paris and served the poor, even taking the place of an innocent man as a galley slave.

___ Father Vincent preached about confession to the people and hundreds of them lined up for confession!

___ Father Vincent started the Sisters of Charity to help serve more of the poor.

___ Priests came out to serve the poor country people with Father Vincent.

Activity - Retelling

See the directions in the Publisher's Preface about how to perform a retelling.

Retell the story in your own words.

Activity - Illustration

Illustrate the picture below of St. Vincent de Paul.